GEORGE GERSHWIN

THREE PRELUDES
FOR PIANO

Edited by Brendan Fox and Richard Walters

GERSHWIN® and GEORGE GERSHWIN®
are registered trademarks of Gershwin Enterprises

ISBN 978-1-5400-3888-3

Visit Hal Leonard Online at
www.halleonard.com

Contact us:
Hal Leonard
7777 West Bluemound Road
Milwaukee, WI 53213
Email: info@halleonard.com

In Europe, contact:
Hal Leonard Europe Limited
42 Wigmore Street
Marylebone, London, W1U 2RN
Email: info@halleonardeurope.com

In Australia, contact:
Hal Leonard Australia Pty. Ltd.
4 Lentara Court
Cheltenham, Victoria, 3192 Australia
Email: info@halleonard.com.au

George Gershwin, c. 1925.
(Photo by Hulton Archive/Getty Images)

PREFACE

In the year 1926, George Gershwin (1898–1937) was riding high on the recent successes of *Rhapsody in Blue* (1924) and the Concerto in F (1925), two trailblazing concert works that integrated jazz styles into large-scale forms. Already known as a composer of popular songs and Broadway musicals, Gershwin now had footing in the world of concert music, with the public eager to follow his next experiment. On December 4, 1926, he premiered five new preludes for piano at the Roosevelt Hotel in New York City, sharing the bill with a contralto singer, who included some of Gershwin's songs. The program also featured two-piano arrangements of the popular *Rhapsody* and the last movement of the Concerto in F. This was an opportunity for Gershwin to show his versatility as a pianist-composer, a sensitive collaborator and soloist who could write brilliantly for his instrument.

Three of the preludes on that December 4 program (and in subsequent performances in Buffalo and Boston) were the ones we know today as Preludes I–III. Based on descriptions from some critics' reviews, the other two preludes were likely the pieces now labeled as "Sleepless Night," a slow blues-inflected number, and "Short Story," a combination of fragments titled "Novelette in Fourths" and "Sixteen Bars Without a Name" (which Gershwin had also arranged for violin and piano). Despite the charm and quality of these other two pieces, Gershwin chose only to publish the first three in 1927. He had apparently planned to write a cycle of 24 preludes titled "The Melting Pot," in the tradition of Chopin, but his increasing activity in the music scene and his tragic early death meant that this effort never came to fruition. Fortunately, *Three Preludes* became wildly popular, with countless performances and dozens of arrangements for various instruments or ensembles, continuing to today.

Since Gershwin himself oversaw and approved the first published edition of *Three Preludes* from New World/Harms, Inc., it represents the most authentic complete source, but we felt it necessary to also study manuscript sources at the Library of Congress. Our editorial decisions are stated in the "Notes." Gershwin's own recordings of the pieces were also enlightening to study. His tempos were notably fast, particularly in Prelude II, and he made some in-the-moment choices to alter rhythms or add ornaments, very much in the spirit of jazz performance.

Brendan Fox and Richard Walters
editors
April 2019

CONTENTS

All fingerings are editorial suggestions except those in italics, which originate with Gershwin.
Other editorial suggestions appear in brackets in this edition.

SOURCES

N   New World Edition (Harms Inc.), 1927

C   Copyist manuscript piano score. George and Ira Gershwin collection, 1895-2008.
Library of Congress. Washington, D.C.

R   Audio recording, 8 June 1928. Gershwin, George. "Three Preludes." *Gershwin plays Gershwin*.
By George Gershwin. Victrola American historic first recordings. RCA Victrola AVM1-1740.

B^{II}   Prelude II, Audio recording, 1932. New York, NBC, Rudy Vallée "Fleischman Hour",
10 November 1932; issued in 1991 as "Gershwin Performs Gershwin," MusicMasters 5062-2-C.

H^{III}   Prelude III, George Gershwin holograph manuscript piano score, incomplete.
George and Ira Gershwin collection, 1895-2008. Library of Congress. Washington, D.C.

M^{III}   Prelude III, manuscript piano score, incomplete. George and Ira Gershwin collection, 1895–2008.
Library of Congress. Washington, D.C.

Also consulted:

A   Alfred Edition, ed. Maurice Hinson, 2006

U   G. Henle Verlag Urtext Edition, ed. Norbert Gertsch, 2008

NOTES

The New World Edition (**N**) was our primary source.
Comments about details from other sources follow below.

PRELUDE I

m. 13, R.H.: We have preserved the slur ending on the first tied A-flat as in **N**, **A**, **U**, and **C**.

m. 15, L.H.: **N**, **A**, and **U** indicate a clearing of the pedal, though **C** does not (possibly an omission).

m. 22, R.H., beat 2: **C** notates this figure as sixteenths. Since the rhythm of the last four notes as thirty-seconds was corrected for **N**, the first edition, the notation of sixteenths in **C** is a mistake. The accent on R.H. beat 2, as well as f, are from **C**.

m. 23, R.H.: See note on m. 13.

m. 25, R.H., beat 1: In **N**, **A**, **U**, and **C**, occurrences of this same figure in mm. 16, 32, and 37 have an accent on the first note.

mm. 30–31: In **C**, the decrescendo ends in the middle of m. 30, beat 2. **N**, **A**, and **U** extend the marking to the last R.H. note in m. 31.

mm. 32–34: Gershwin's performance in **R** supports the case that the p marking is only for the notes in the L.H.

m. 35: The suggested p for the L.H. is not from any source, but implied by preceding measures.

m. 37: No dynamic markings in any source. We have suggested the same mf and p dynamics as m. 32. Gershwin's performance in **R** supports this choice.

m. 43: The crescendo hairpin in **C** is loosely drawn and could be interpreted as ending at the E-flat in beat 2 in the R.H., but **N**, **A**, and **U** carry it to the end of the measure.

mm. 46–47: In beat 1 in the R.H., **C** has an up-stemmed A octave and C octave respectively, rather than the full chords in **N**, **A**, and **U**.

mm. 46–49: Some regular accents in **C** were changed to staccato accents in **N**, **A**, and **U**.

mm. 50–53: Gershwin rewrote these measures before the first edition. **C** shows:

mm. 54–57: **C** has no slurs in the R.H., but these were added in **N**.

mm. 59–60: **C** has no accents in the offbeats of the L.H., though they are present in similar figures in mm. 54–58. Accents were added in **N**.

m. 62: In **R**, Gershwin delays the last L.H. note slightly, a spontaneous performance choice.

PRELUDE II

m. 2: We have matched **C** in placement of the *legato* mark in m. 2, meaning a continuation of the slurring in m. 1. **N** has the slur and *legato* in m. 1, and nothing in m. 2.

m. 7: On Gershwin's recording, **R**, he plays grace note B-sharps in the R.H. leading up to the C-sharps, probably spontaneous performance choices.

m. 8, beat 2, R.H.: The slur was not present in **C**, but was added for the first edition.

m. 9, beat 4, L.H.: **C** does not have a natural on the B, corrected in the first edition, also corrected in m. 23.

m. 11, beat 1, R.H.: **C** notates the grace notes as eighths, but these were changed to sixteenths in the first edition.

m. 14: The brackets in the L.H. are from **N**. A pianist might choose to play the L.H.'s top voice in beats 1, 3, and 4 in the R.H.

m. 18: In **C**, the *legato* mark is placed on beat 1 of m. 19, but **N** places it at the R.H. entrance.

mm. 26–28: **C** has no slurs over the R.H. phrases, but slurs were added in **N**.

m. 31: "Optional version: reverse hands" is not in **C**, added in **N**. Gershwin himself likely played the passage from m. 31–44 with hands reversed. In **R**, Gershwin plays the final R.H. C-sharp in m. 30 as an upbeat to the beginning of the melody, continuing in the lower staff in m. 31.

mm. 33–34: In **R**, Gershwin continues to swing the L.H. eighth notes. In **B**^{II} (the 1932 recording) he plays an altered rhythm.

m. 44: In **B**^{II}, Gershwin plays an additional chord in the R.H. on beat 2, not in any printed source.

m. 45: See comment on m. 1.

m. 52: See comment on m. 14.

PRELUDE III

m. 2: **C** and **M**^{III} do not have a natural sign on the C in the L.H. chord in beat 1, but a natural was added for the first edition. Gershwin plays a C-natural in his 1928 recording (**R**).

m. 4: The idiosyncratic notation in beat 2 in the R.H. suggests that the R.H. takes the A-flat and holds it while playing the C-flat. This bracket is present in sources **N**, **C**, and **M**^{III}.

m. 5: **H**^{III}, which does not include mm. 1–4, has a tempo marking of **Agitato**, not adopted in subsequent sources. The first edition states *a tempo*, a return to the opening **Allegro ben rimato e deciso**.

mm 5, 7, 13–15: **H**^{III} has different articulations than sources **N**, **C**, and **M**^{III} on the L.H. notes: in mm. 5–7, staccato-tenuto instead of staccato-staccato; in 13–15, staccato-tenuto instead of staccato-accent/staccato.

m. 16: In **H**^{III}, the D-flats in both hands in beat 1 are tied to beat 2, over a half-note bass note.

mm. 17–20: **H**^{III} has the R.H. notes transposed up an octave and different material in the L.H. This was not adopted in future sources.

m. 20: In **C** and **M**^{III}, the thirty-second notes on beat 1 are notated with the first B-flat and A-flat together in a chord. In **N**, this was changed to a septuplet.

m. 25: The *tenuto* is for the L.H. chord. M^{III} has a *tenuto* marking on the L.H. chord on beat 2.

mm. 34–36, 42–45: The chords are not arpeggiated in C. C has slurs on only two of the four R.H. triplet phrases. Slurs were added in N.

m. 42: The crescendo is not in C or N, suggested to match m. 34.

mm. 47–48: C has no arpeggio marks that are present in N. In R, Gershwin actually plays these chords unarpeggiated.

m. 49: In R, Gershwin plays the L.H. chord on beat 1 as a B-flat octave rather than a chord, and does not play the D in the R.H.

m. 50: In R, Gershwin does not play the L.H. B-flat on beat 2.

mm. 52, 54, 56: In M^{III}, the upstemmed quarter-note chord in the R.H. is dotted in m. 52, not dotted in m. 54, and mm. 55–57 are left blank and marked (a), (b), (c) for mm. 51–53 to be copied out. In C, these chords on beat 1 are dotted in m. 52 and 56, but not 54, taking Gershwin's marks literally. In N these three chords are quarter notes followed by an eighth rest.

GEORGE GERSHWIN
THREE PRELUDES
FOR PIANO

To Bill Daly

Prelude I

George Gershwin

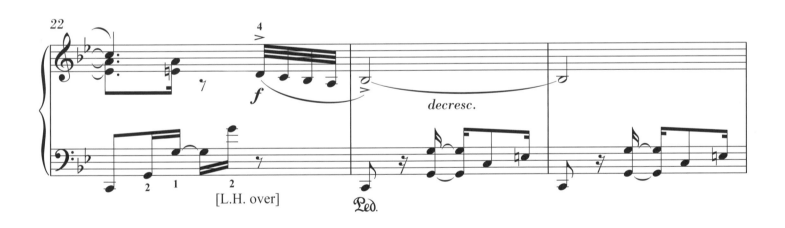

[L.H. over R.H.]

Prelude II

George Gershwin

Andante con moto e poco rubato (♩ = 88)

*The brackets are from the sources. However, it may be easier to play the top notes in the bass clef with the R.H.

optional version: reverse hands

** See comment about m. 10.

Prelude III

George Gershwin

Allegro ben ritmato e deciso (♩ = 116)

sempre stacc.